FORLORN HOPE

Writen &

Illustrated

by

JASIN MOON

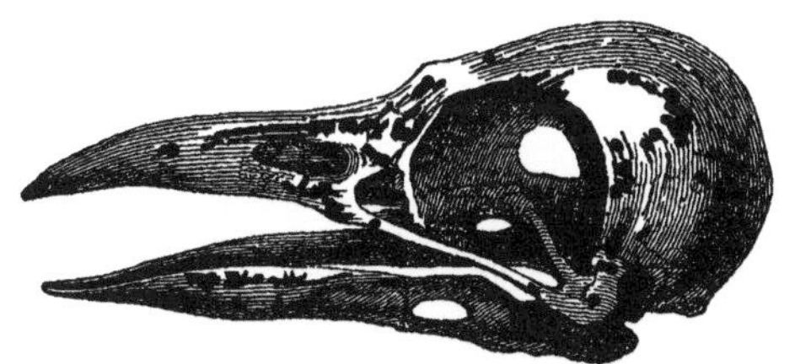

A BOOK OF
MACABRE POETRY
& ART

"I became insane, with long intervals of horrible sanity."

- Edgar Allen Poe

Contents

Introduction: 6

A Specter's Promise: 10

For a Friendship lost: 12

My Dark Companion: 14

A Symphony of Souls: 16

Luna's Glow: 18

A Haunting Reminder: 20

Harbinger of Pain: 22

Cup of Tea: 24

Pricked by a Rose: 26

Forlorn Hope: 28

Lost at Sea: 30

Seasons of a Lifetime: 32

Pain and Solitude: 34

Her Hearts Lament: 36

The Tempter: 38

Nightmare: 40

Abscond from Death 42

We Shall Endure 44

A Spiders Alure 46

Forevermore 48

My Cruel Fate 50

Duality of a Cat 52

In Search of Brains 54

Where Dreams Collid 56

From Shallow Graves 60

In Moonlights Gleam 64

A Desolate Creater 66

A Mysterious Girl 68

The Last Gasp 70

Ode to the Moon 72

INTRODUCTION

THE HAUNTING LITERARY WORKS OF EDGAR ALLEN POE HAS BIRTHED A MESMERISING REALM OF ARTISTIC EXPRESSION IN ME. INTERTWINED WITH MY LOVE OF GOTHIC MUSIC AND MACABRE ART HAS INSPIRED THE WORDS AND IMAGES WITHIN THESE PAGES.

I have drawn inspiration from Poe's tale of the mysterious and the supernatural, delving into the depths of the human psyche, capturing the essence of despair, longing, and the fragility of the human condition.

Through my work, I unravel the intricate threads of the human soul and the darkness that lingers within.

My art is born from the fusion emanates and unsettling allure, invoking a sense of both fascination and trepidation, as it transports me to a realm where the boundaries between reality and the supernatural blur. It is a testament to the enduring powers of Poe words and the evocative force of gothic music, fostering a visual tapestry that delves deep into the realm of the macabre, leaving an indelible mark upon my psyche, and hopefully yours.

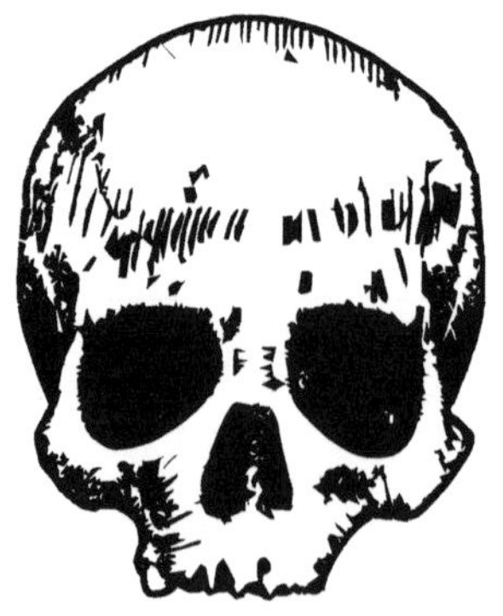

Forlorn Hope

"A persistent or desperate hope that is unlikely to be fulfilled."

A Specter's Promise

In shadows deep, where darkness swells,
A haunting tale my heart foretells,
Within this realm of ghostly gloom,
Caught a glimpse, my soul consumed.

In midnight's grasp, I wandered lost,
Through misty vales where souls were tossed,
The pallid moon, a flickering guide,
I sought solace, but love denied.

Yet, in this realm of deathly hue,
I spied a figure, ethereal and true,
A vision fair, with mournful grace,
A face that held a lover's trace.

Her eyes, twin orbs of starless night,
In them, a flicker, a distant light,
Her pallor cold, like marble stone,
Yet warmed my heart, though all alone.

Ensnared by fate's unyielding hand,
I stood in awe, a haunted man,
For there she stood, in spectral glow,
The love of mine, from long ago.

Her alabaster hair, like death's shroud,
A silken curtain, soft and proud,
A fragile frame, a spectral sight,
A phantom fair, in ghostly white.

As if from sepulchral slumber she rose,
Her voice, a whisper, through the
shadows flows,
A lamentation, a sorrowful moan,
Aching melodies in mournful tone.

Yet, in her eyes, a tender gleam,
A stolen moment, a lover's dream,
Though death's embrace had
claimed her breath,
Her spirit lingered, defying death.

I reached out, my hand in air,
Yearning to touch, to feel her there,
But she dissolved, like misty dew,
A spectre's promise, never to pursue.

Now, I dwell in darkness deep,
Where love and loss forever seep,
And though my heart with sorrow swells,
I'm haunted still by love's cruel spells.

For in that realm, where spirits roam,
I glimpsed the love that I had known,
A phantom's love, forever missed,
A spectre's kiss, forever kissed.

For a Friendship Lost

In darkness dreary, where shadows weep,
A tale I tell, of sorrow deep,
Of friend once held, now lost to sleep,
In the realm where spectres creep.

Once a vibrant soul, like ember bright,
A beacon in the ebony night,
With laughter's warmth, a guiding light,
Now silenced in eternal flight.

The moon, it weeps, its tears do fall,
Upon a grave, where whispers crawl,
An epitaph, a mournful scrawl,
Etched in stone, and funeral pall.

Oh, dear friend, thy spirit gone,
From earthly realm, forever withdrawn,
Yet memories linger, a sombre song,
In my heart, where they belong.

The breeze, it moans, a mournful sigh,
Through twisted branches, reaching high,
A requiem sung, as night draws nigh,
For a friendship lost, that cannot die.

Gone are the days of laughter shared,
In shadowed halls, where secrets bared,
A haunting absence, a void declared,
A wound too deep, for time repaired.

In dreams, we meet, like echoes faint,
In spectral realms, where spirits taint,
A spectral touch, a whispered plaint,
In the realm where memories paint.

Oh, melancholy, thy grasp so tight,
Enshrouded in sorrow's pallid light,
For in my heart, there burns a blight,
In mourning's veil, forever to fight.

And so, dear friend, in realms unknown,
Where spirits wander and hearts have flown,
In death's embrace, you are not alone,
For my love for you shall forever be shown.

My Dark Companion

In the darkness of night my eyes see thee,
My black cat, my companion of old,
Your Fur like the night, your Eyes like the moon,
Your tail like a whip, your paws like a mold.

You sit by the fire, watching me as I write,
Your eyes never blinking, your gaze never stray,
Your head cocked to one side, as if to say,
"What are you writing about, my human today?"

I don't know what I'm writing about, my cat,
But I know that it's something full of despair,
Something that will make your fur stand on end,
Something that will make you hiss and spit and swear.

But you will stay with me, my black cat,
You will sit by the fire and watch me write,
And when I am finished, you will rub my face,
And purr your approval of my dark and twisted might.

A SYMPHONY OF SOULS

Within shadows deep, where secrets dwell,
There walked a man, his story to tell.
A soul divided, torn in twain,
One side in light, the other in disdain.

With hesitant steps, he ventured forth,
Embracing darkness, seeking its worth.
For in his heart, a curious yearning,
To understand the depths of his own churning.

His dark half lurked, a phantom near,
Whispering doubts into his ear.
Yet the man pressed on, undeterred,
In his quest to bridge the divide, unperturbed.

In moonlit nights, they met and spoke,
Two entities entwined, an unusual cloak.
Their conversations danced in twilight's embrace,
Revealing truths, as masks slipped from each face.

The man discovered strength in his dark twin,
A reservoir of courage dwelling within.
For shadows hold wisdom, secrets untold,
A treasure trove hidden from light's stronghold.

Together they roamed, through valleys of despair,
Navigating storms with a fearless air.
The dark half tempered, a tempest's fire,
Guiding the man through his deepest quagmire.

In time, they forged an unlikely bond,
A friendship deep, forever beyond.
For the man realised, in accepting his duality,
He found the essence of his own vitality.

Through their union, a balance was struck,
No longer at odds, no longer stuck.
Both light and dark now danced in harmony,
A symphony of souls, forever free.

So let us learn from this tale's decree,
To embrace our shadows, set them free.
For within the darkness, light does reside,
And in befriending our dark halves,
we truly thrive.

Luna's Light

A Lullaby for the Damned

CLOAKED BY NIGHT, THE MOON AWAKES,

A SPECTRAL PRESENCE, HAUNTINGLY OPAQUE.

A SILENT WITNESS TO SHADOWS' DANCE,

IT CASTS ITS GAZE WITH A CHILLING GLANCE.

OH, LUNAR MISTRESS, ETHEREAL AND PALE,

YOU WEAVE YOUR WEB, AN EERIE VEIL.

A BEACON OF DARKNESS, A HARBINGER

OF WOE, YOU GUIDE THE LOST,

WHERE SECRETS GROW.

YOUR FACE, A MASK OF MELANCHOLY,

REFLECTING SORROW, DEEP AND UNHOLY.

WITH EACH PHASE, A TALE UNFOLDS,

OF SHATTERED DREAMS AND STORIES UNTOLD.

BEWARE THE MOON'S SEDUCTIVE LIGHT,

FOR IT CONCEALS THE HORRORS OF THE NIGHT.

IT BECKONS CREATURES OF DARKNESS NEAR,

WHISPERING SECRETS THAT MORTALS FEAR.

BATHED IN YOUR GLOW, THE WORLD TRANSFORMS,

TWISTED ILLUSIONS, WHERE DARKNESS SWARMS.

A HAUNTED VISAGE IN THE SKY ABOVE,

CASTING ITS SPELL, A CURSE TO ALL WHO LOVE.

THE MOON, A SPECTRE IN THE ENDLESS ABYSS,

A MIRROR TO THE VOID, WHERE DARKNESS PERSISTS.

ITS BEAUTY HIDES A MACABRE SYMPHONY,

A LULLABY FOR THE DAMNED, A MOURNFUL MELODY.

SO AS THE MOON ASCENDS, ITS WATCH BEGUN,

BEWARE THE SECRETS IT KEEPS, THE BATTLES WON.

FOR IN THE DEPTHS OF ITS COLD EMBRACE,

LIE THE ECHOES OF SORROW,

IN A SHADOWY SPACE.

A Haunting Reminder

On this sombre night, as spirits softly weep,
A tale unfolds, a love buried deep.
Through the mist and gloom, a heart's despair,
A macabre desire, beyond life's snare.

In the depths of my grave, where darkness dwells,
A fervent yearning, a forbidden spell.
With fingers skeletal, I claw the earth,
Seeking release, a morbid rebirth.

Through soil's embrace, my hands emerge,
A ghastly sight, my soul's cruel surge.
Determined to break free from death's cold hold,
To taste the lips of the one I long to behold.

With each inch I rise, an ache in my bones,
Seeking the love that only death disowns.
Through the tombstones' shadows,
I stumble forth,
A spectre defying mortality's worth.

Her beauty, a memory etched in my mind,
A love transcending the realms of mankind.
Through the veils of decay, I persist,
Yearning to hold her, my ethereal tryst.

Finally, I reach the world of the living,
A ghostly apparition, unforgiving.
Yet, I press on, for love knows no bounds,
Even in death, passion resounds.

In the moonlit garden, where she awaits,
My beloved fair, untouched by cruel fates.
I draw near, a spectre with love's intent,
To kiss her lips, though my flesh is rent.

Our lips meet, a union of life and death,
A macabre embrace, where passions take breath.
In that moment, time ceases its cruel flow,
As our love transcends both realms we know.

But alas, the dawn creeps upon the land,
My time fleeting,
slipping through death's hand.
Back to the grave, I must descend,
A bittersweet ending, a love condemned.

In the cold earth, my slumber resumes,
Dreaming of kisses amidst graves and tombs.
For even in death, our love does persist,
A haunting reminder, in eternal mist.

HARBINGER OF PAIN

ON THE SHADOWED REALM WHERE DARKNESS THRIVES,
A TALE UNFOLDS OF TWISTED LIVES.
A CROW, THE HARBINGER, WITH FEATHERS BLACK,
UNFURLS ITS WINGS, A CRUEL ATTACK.

ON MIDNIGHT'S BREEZE, IT GLIDES WITH GRACE,
SEARCHING FOR SOULS TO CLAIM AND CHASE.
WITH EYES LIKE ONYX, COLD AND KEEN,
IT PREYS UPON HEARTS THAT LOVE CONVENE.

THROUGH MOONLIT WOODS, ITS CRIES RESOUND,
A HAUNTING CALL, A MOURNFUL SOUND.
THE CROW'S DARK SILHOUETTE ENGULFS THE NIGHT,
AS IT SEEKS ITS PREY WITH RELENTLESS MIGHT.

BEWARE, OH LOVER, OF THE CROW'S CRUEL SONG,
FOR IT LURES YOU CLOSE, WHERE SHADOWS BELONG.
WITH A CHARM DISGUISED, IT CAPTIVATES YOUR SOUL,
PULLING YOU IN WITH A DARKNESS UNTOLD.

ITS WINGS ENFOLD, A RAVEN'S EMBRACE,
WHISPERING PROMISES, IN WHISPERS LACED.
INTO THE ABYSS, IT CARRIES YOU AWAY,
LEAVING BEHIND A WORLD TURNED GREY.

THE LOVER, LOST, IN THE CROW'S CRUEL GRIP,
FADES INTO THE NIGHT, LIKE A SINKING SHIP.
NEVERMORE TO FEEL THE WARMTH OF DAY,
FOREVER ENTWINED IN THE CROW'S TWISTED PLAY.

OH, MOURNFUL CROW, WITH BEADY EYES SO KEEN,
YOU STEAL THEIR HEARTS, THEIR LOVE UNSEEN.
IN YOUR EBONY FEATHERS, SECRETS RESIDE,
AS YOU SOAR THROUGH DARKNESS, WITH LOVE DENIED.

SO HEED THE WARNING, OH HEARTS THAT YEARN,
FOR THE CROW'S ALLURE, A TWISTED TURN.
LEST YOU SUCCUMB TO ITS WICKED EMBRACE,
AND FIND YOUR LOVE LOST IN ETERNAL CHASE.

FOR IN THE REALM WHERE SHADOWS REIGN,
THE CROW PERSISTS, A HARBINGER OF PAIN.
A LOVE STOLEN AWAY, FOREVER TO ROAM,
IN THE CLUTCHES OF THE CROW, A HEARTLESS HOME.

A CUP OF TEA

Beneath the cloak of darkness, 'neath a moon aglow,
In a forest deep and ancient, where secrets often grow,
Three witches gathered, their powers all aligned,
To share a cup of sorcery, a moment so divine.

Their cauldron simmered, whispered ancient tales,
Of spells and incantations, of triumphs and travails,
In whispered words, their voices wove a spell,
And nature listened, enraptured, to
the stories they would tell.

The first witch, with eyes of ember and hair of raven's hue,
Brought wisdom and foresight, her visions crystal true.
She poured the tea, a brew of dreams and distant past,
An elixir of enchantment, memories meant to last.

The second witch, adorned in moonlight's silver gleam,
With fingers nimble, conjured magic like a dream.
She stirred the cup with moonbeams, a celestial dance,
Infusing it with starlight and a touch of wild romance.

THE THIRD WITCH, CLOAKED IN SHADOW, AN AIR OF MYSTERY,
ADDED HERBS OF ANCIENT POWER, GRANTING LIFE'S SWEET MYSTERY.
SHE WHISPERED SECRET INCANTATIONS, A
GIFT FROM REALMS UNKNOWN,
AND WITH EACH WORD, THE TEA TRANSFORMED,
ITS ESSENCE DEEPLY SOWN.

TOGETHER THEY SIPPED, THEIR SENSES INTERTWINED,
IN THE STILLNESS OF THE FOREST, THEIR SPIRITS COMBINED.
THEY TASTED DREAMS AND VISIONS, THE FUTURE YET UNTOLD,
AS THE MOONLIGHT BATHED THEM, ITS SILVER MAGIC BOLD.

EACH SIP BROUGHT FORTH THEIR POWERS, ENHANCED AND BRIGHT,
AWAKENING ANCIENT FORCES, ILLUMINATING THE NIGHT.
THEIR LAUGHTER ECHOED THROUGH THE TREES, A HARMONY SO RARE,
AS THEY REVELLED IN THE MAGIC, A SISTERHOOD THEY SHARE.

UNDER THE WATCHFUL MOON, THEY WOVE
THEIR SPELLS SO FINE,
BINDING PAST AND PRESENT, WEAVING FUTURE'S DESIGN.
IN THAT MYSTICAL MOMENT, THEIR TEA A SACRED KEY,
THREE WITCHES MET IN UNITY, BOUND BY DESTINY.

SO NEXT TIME YOU WANDER 'NEATH THE MOON'S
ENCHANTING GAZE, REMEMBER THE WITCHES' MEETING,
THE FOREST'S MYSTIC HAZE.
FOR IN THE CUP OF TEA, A TOUCH OF MAGIC LIES,
WHERE DREAMS AND SECRETS MINGLE, UNDER MOONLIT SKIES.

Pricked By a Rose

In shadowed gardens, where roses fair reside,
A temptress dwells, with petals as crimson tides.
Her beauty, a raven's wing in moonlit gloom,
Beckons with allure, ensnaring me in her bloom.

Oh, sweet enchantress, with fragrant grace unfurled,
Thy velvety touch, a vision to the world.
Yet beware, dear soul, of her beguiling call,
For her thorns conceal a cruel fate to befall.

I yearn to hold her, this blossom of desire,
To taste her nectar, set my spirit afire.
But as my trembling hand draws near her embrace,
Her thorns extend, eager to leave their trace.

A fleeting touch, a mere caress so slight,
But the rose, jealous mistress, doth incite
A crimson stain upon my tender skin,
As though the gods themselves revel in sin.

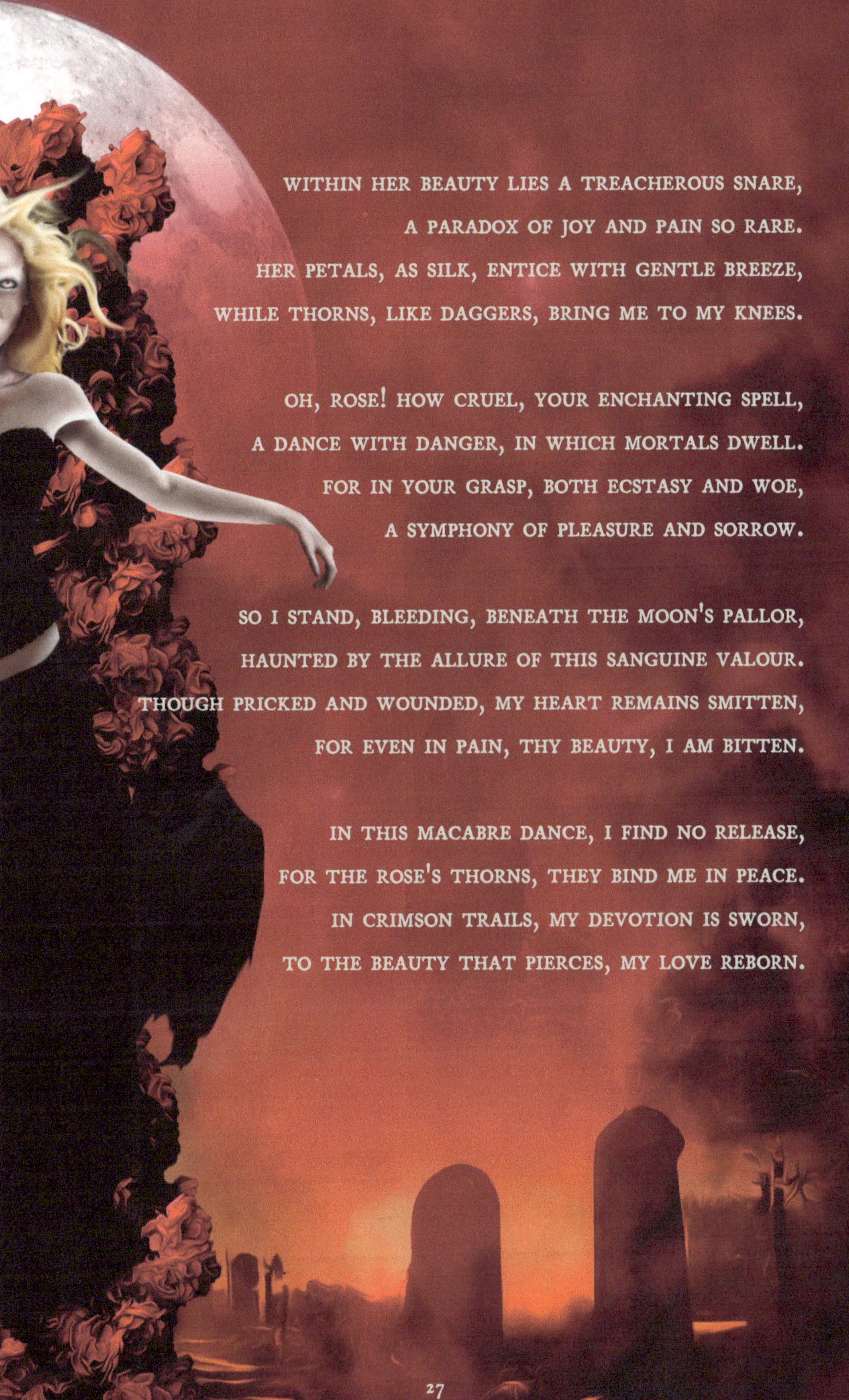

WITHIN HER BEAUTY LIES A TREACHEROUS SNARE,
A PARADOX OF JOY AND PAIN SO RARE.
HER PETALS, AS SILK, ENTICE WITH GENTLE BREEZE,
WHILE THORNS, LIKE DAGGERS, BRING ME TO MY KNEES.

OH, ROSE! HOW CRUEL, YOUR ENCHANTING SPELL,
A DANCE WITH DANGER, IN WHICH MORTALS DWELL.
FOR IN YOUR GRASP, BOTH ECSTASY AND WOE,
A SYMPHONY OF PLEASURE AND SORROW.

SO I STAND, BLEEDING, BENEATH THE MOON'S PALLOR,
HAUNTED BY THE ALLURE OF THIS SANGUINE VALOUR.
THOUGH PRICKED AND WOUNDED, MY HEART REMAINS SMITTEN,
FOR EVEN IN PAIN, THY BEAUTY, I AM BITTEN.

IN THIS MACABRE DANCE, I FIND NO RELEASE,
FOR THE ROSE'S THORNS, THEY BIND ME IN PEACE.
IN CRIMSON TRAILS, MY DEVOTION IS SWORN,
TO THE BEAUTY THAT PIERCES, MY LOVE REBORN.

Forlorn Hope

In the depths of my soul, a lament does reside,

A tale of love's struggle, with passion denied.

Forlorn hope, aching heart, I cast my gaze afar,

Wondering if love's flame will ever rise like a star.

In this world so jaded, where cynicism thrives,

The future of love seems scarce, like forgotten hives.

Passion's embers flicker, dimming with each passing day,

As apathy and indifference lead hearts astray.

Once, love danced in gardens, vibrant and alive,

Where tender hearts entwined, no fear to contrive.

But now, in desolate landscapes, love's blooms have withered,

As doubts and disillusionment leave spirits dithered.

Will passion be rekindled, in a world so cold and stark?

Or shall it remain a relic, lost in shadows dark?

I yearn for love's revival, its flame to burn anew,

But despair whispers softly, "Love's future is askew."

YET, IN THE DEPTHS OF MY BEING, A GLIMMER REMAINS,

A STEADFAST BELIEF THAT LOVE TRANSCENDS ALL PAINS.

FOR IN THE FACE OF ADVERSITY, LOVE'S STRENGTH DOES SOAR,

ITS RESILIENCE UNYIELDING, FOREVER SEEKING MORE.

SO LET US NOT SURRENDER TO DESPAIR'S BITTER PLEA,

BUT RALLY THE HOPE WITHIN US, SET OUR SPIRITS FREE.

FOR LOVE'S FUTURE LIES IN OUR HANDS,

HEARTS INTERTWINED,

AS WE CULTIVATE COMPASSION,

LOVE'S TRUE ESSENCE WE FIND.

IN THE DARKEST OF MOMENTS, WHEN ALL SEEMS AMISS,

LOVE'S LIGHT WILL GUIDE US, THROUGH THE ABYSS.

WITH COURAGE AS OUR COMPASS,

WE'LL FORGE A PATH ANEW,

RESURRECTING LOVE'S PASSION,

STEADFAST AND TRUE.

FORLORN HOPE MAY HAUNT US, BUT IT SHALL NOT PREVAIL,

AS LONG AS HEARTS BEAT, LOVE'S TRIUMPH WE'LL UNVEIL.

LET US NURTURE THE FLAMES, WITH TENDERNESS AND CARE,

AND RECLAIM THE FUTURE OF LOVE, A STORY WE'LL SHARE.

Lost at Sea

In the depths of darkness, I wander, lost and alone,
Where shadows dance upon the forsaken stone.
A spectral veil wraps around my weary soul,
As whispers of despair take their solemn toll.

In this forsaken realm, where hope has fled,
I stumble, haunted by a relentless dread.
My eyes, the only windows to a world so cruel,
Witness scenes of joy, of passion and renewal.

I see them there, a tapestry of bliss,
Laughter echoing, like a sweet, venomous hiss.
Their faces aglow, with love's radiant embrace,
But I remain an outsider, bound in this desolate space.

Their smiles, like daggers, pierce my fragile heart,
A cruel reminder that I'm set apart.
I yearn to feel the warmth of love's embrace,
But destiny has deemed me unworthy of such grace.

I AM A GHOST, A PHANTOM IN THE NIGHT,
CONDEMNED TO WATCH, HIDDEN FROM THEIR SIGHT.
THE WORLD WHIRLS BY, IN A SYMPHONY OF DELIGHT,
YET I'M CONDEMNED TO DWELL IN ETERNAL NIGHT.

SILENT TEARS CASCADE DOWN MY WEARY CHEEKS,
AS I YEARN FOR SOLACE, FOR THE SOLACE THAT LIFE SEEKS.
BUT FATE HAS WOVEN A TAPESTRY OF SORROW AND WOE,
AND IN THIS REALM OF DARKNESS, I AM FORCED TO FOREGO.

SO I WANDER, LOST, A SPECTRE IN DESPAIR,
IN THIS TWILIGHT REALM WHERE HOPE IS RARE.
I WATCH THE DANCE OF LIFE WITH HOLLOW EYES,
A SILENT WITNESS TO LOVE'S CRUEL DEMISE.

IN THIS DESOLATE VOID, I AM FOREVER CONFINED,
TO WITNESS THEIR JOY, THEIR LAUGHTER ENTWINED.
ALONE IN THE DARKNESS, FOREVER LEFT TO BE,
A WRETCHED SOUL, FORSAKEN, LOST AT SEA.

Seasons of a Lifetime

In Spring's tender embrace, a life begins,
As blossoms bloom, new hope takes flight.
A man is born, amidst nature's wings,
A soul awakening, bathed in golden light.

Through verdant meadows, he starts to grow,
In Summer's fervour, his youth takes hold.
With each radiant sunrise and sunset's glow,
His spirit ignites, fearless and bold.

As the sun blazes high in the azure sky,
His heart blossoms with dreams anew.
He dances with joy, chasing butterflies,
Exploring the world, embracing the true.

But Autumn's whisper brings a change untold,
Leaves ablaze in hues of amber and red.
Love finds its way, as fate gently unfolds,
And the man, now a groom, shares vows to be wed.

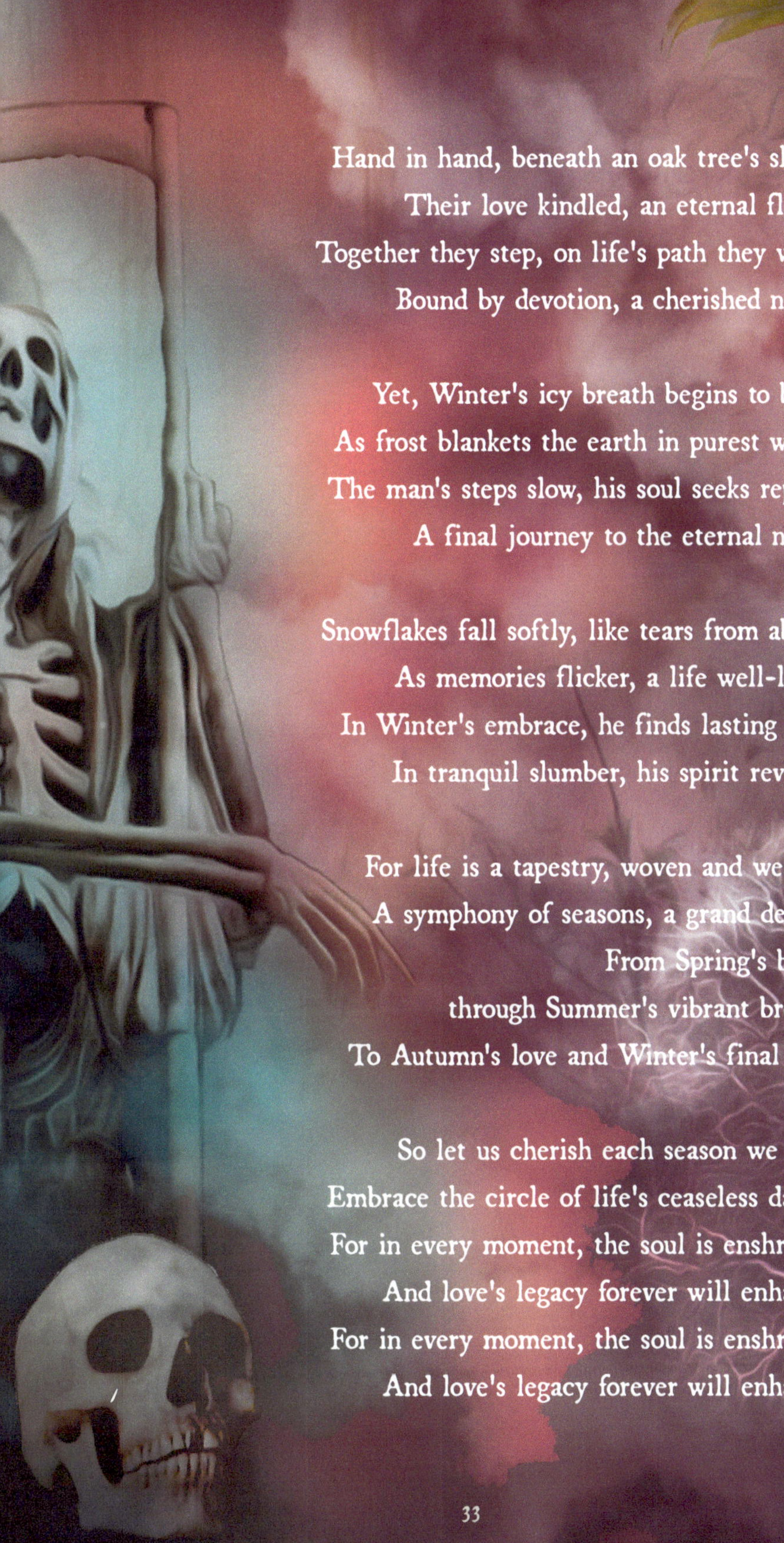

Hand in hand, beneath an oak tree's shade,
Their love kindled, an eternal flame.
Together they step, on life's path they wade,
Bound by devotion, a cherished name.

Yet, Winter's icy breath begins to blow,
As frost blankets the earth in purest white.
The man's steps slow, his soul seeks repose,
A final journey to the eternal night.

Snowflakes fall softly, like tears from above,
As memories flicker, a life well-lived.
In Winter's embrace, he finds lasting love,
In tranquil slumber, his spirit revived.

For life is a tapestry, woven and weaved,
A symphony of seasons, a grand design.
From Spring's birth,
through Summer's vibrant breeze,
To Autumn's love and Winter's final line.

So let us cherish each season we find,
Embrace the circle of life's ceaseless dance.
For in every moment, the soul is enshrined,
And love's legacy forever will enhance.
For in every moment, the soul is enshrined,
And love's legacy forever will enhance.

PAIN AND SOLITUDE

In the chamber's darkest corner, he sits,
A man, burdened by life's relentless twists,
With weary eyes and a heavy heart's beat,
He contemplates the cruelty life did unleash.

His soul entangled in sorrow's bitter embrace,
Haunted by memories, bound in eternal chase,
Alone, he ponders the spectre of his past,
As shadows dance, a morbid spell they cast.

Through the silence, a whisper, faint and low,
Echoes of a lost lover, from realms below,
Her voice, like a feather, brushes his ear,
"I forgive you," she whispers, wiping his tear.

Tears well up in his eyes, a torrent of pain,
A flood of longing, a love he can't regain,
Her ethereal presence, a bittersweet balm,
Yet cruel reminder of his eternal qualm.

Hand in hand, beneath an oak tree's shade,
Their love kindled, an eternal flame.
Together they step, on life's path they wade,
Bound by devotion, a cherished name.

Yet, Winter's icy breath begins to blow,
As frost blankets the earth in purest white.
The man's steps slow, his soul seeks repose,
A final journey to the eternal night.

Snowflakes fall softly, like tears from above,
As memories flicker, a life well-lived.
In Winter's embrace, he finds lasting love,
In tranquil slumber, his spirit revived.

A symphony of seasons, a grand design.
From Spring's birth,
through Summer's vibrant breeze,
To Autumn's love and
Winter's final line.

So let us cherish each season we find,
Embrace the circle of life's ceaseless dance.
For in every moment, the soul is enshrined,
And love's legacy forever will enhance.
For in every moment, the soul is enshrined,
And love's legacy forever will enhance.

HER HEARTS LAMENT

On a somber night, a girl did stray,
Lost in a world where darkness held sway,
A solitary soul, burdened and forlorn,
In a realm where hope had long been torn.

She wandered aimlessly, her heart's lament,
Through twisted paths and corridors bent,
No solace found in the cold, desolate night,
Her spirit waned, consumed by blight.

Through murky woods, she ventured deep,
Where whispers of sorrow would forever creep,
An ethereal fog embraced her weary frame,
As despair whispered secrets, branding her name.

Yet in the distance, a glimmer so faint,
A beacon of light, a flicker to paint,
A tunnel emerged from the void's cruel might,
A slender path leading her to respite.

The girl, fragile and filled with despair,
Followed the glow with a desperate prayer,
Each step a struggle, her legs heavy as lead,
Yet driven by a longing to escape dread.

The tunnel loomed, its walls adorned,
With ancient symbols of souls reborn,
But darkness clawed and threatened to smother,
The light of hope, her tether to another.

Yet she pressed on, defying fate's decree,
Her heart ablaze with tenacity,
Through whispers of spirits and eerie moans,
She traversed the tunnel, her soul in zones.

As she drew closer, the light grew bright,
Illuminating the depths, dispelling the night,
Her fragile form bathed in its gentle embrace,
A shimmering warmth, a holy grace.

And there, at the end, a world anew,
A realm where dreams and fantasies grew,
A paradise birthed from her spirit's strife,
A sanctuary where darkness took no life.

In that moment, the girl's eyes did gleam,
With the promise of joy, like a long-lost dream,
For in the darkest depths, hope still thrived,
Guiding her soul to a realm revived.

No longer lost, no longer alone,
She found solace in a world yet unknown,
A testament to the strength of her will,
To rise from despair and darkness still.

So, dear wanderer, when shadows entwine,
And solitude's grip leaves no hope to find,
Remember the girl, her journey so grand,
And the light at the tunnel's end,
 outstretched hand.

THE TEMPTER

In darkness deep, where whispers thrive,
A man did tread, his soul alive.
With weary eyes, and burdened heart,
He sought respite from life's cruel art.

Beside the grave, a stranger stood,
His tongue a serpent, tempting food.
With honeyed words, he cast his spell,
A macabre dance, where demons dwell.

"Embrace the void," the tempter said,
"Release your worries, fears be shed.
For in this tomb, eternal peace,
A refuge sweet, where anguish cease."

The man, beguiled, his reason lost,
Embraced the grave at such great cost.
Like Sirens' song, the tempter's lies,
Pulled him deeper, 'neath somber skies.

Each whispered verse, a poison dart,
Injected deep into his heart.
His dreams and hopes, all turned to dust,
As darkness claimed his every trust.

"Let go of love, its chains confine,
In cold embrace, your soul entwine.
For passion's fire burns, too bright,
Consume yourself, banish the light."

The man, entrapped in sorrow's snare,
Traded his joy for deep despair.
He dug his grave with trembling hands,
A willing slave to Fate's demands.

And as the earth consumed his frame,
The tempter laughed, his wicked game.
For in the end, the man did find,
No solace true, no peace of mind.

A cautionary tale, this dark lament,
Of voices tempting man's descent.
Beware the tongues that lead astray,
And seek the light, in truth, to stay.

NIGHTMARE

Amongst twilight realm where shadows dance,
There dwells a man in a fateful trance,
Haunted by a nightmare, a phantom course,
A horse of darkness with eyes aflame, remorse.

Once, in a moment of misguided desire,
He traded his soul for fleeting empire,
A pact made in whispers, a devil's toll,
Now his heart quivers, burdened by guilt's coal.

Through misty moors and moonlit lanes,
The nightmarish steed, tormenting reins,
With hooves that thunder, pounding dread,
The horse of fire, the man's soul bled.

Its eyes, like embers, burning deep,
Piercing his conscience, waking from sleep,
The flames devour his dreams and peace,
A haunting reminder of a soul's release.

In every waking hour, he feels the weight,
Of remorse's chains, a relentless fate,
For greed's temptation, he fell too fast,
Now, his soul's ashes scattered in the past.

Within the depths of his weary soul,
He yearns for redemption, to make him whole,
But the horse of nightmares won't let go,
Its fiery gaze, an eternal woe.

He wanders in shadows, seeking the light,
Begging forgiveness in the darkest night,
His heart, a tempest, drowning in pain,
Seeking solace, hoping to break the chain.

Yet, in the depths of his haunted plight,
A flicker of hope, a glimmering light,
For guilt's burden can be a guiding fire,
Leading him back from the abyss's mire.

Through sorrow's valley, he'll find his way,
To mend the fragments of his soul's decay,
With remorse as his compass, he'll strive,
To reclaim his spirit, so he may survive.

In the darkest hour, redemption's call,
A chance to rise, to stand tall,
He'll face the burning eyes that haunt,
And with courage, finally confront.

For guilt can be the path to grace,
A catalyst for a new embrace,
The man, once burdened by his sinful toll,
Shall find salvation and reclaim his soul.

Abscond from Death

Here is a woman who defied Death's claim,
With fervent hope, she played a daring game.
Seeking immortality, she hid from the cold,
In pursuit of a destiny yet untold.

In shadows deep, she sought eternal youth,
A timeless beauty, everlasting truth.
With every breath, she yearned to break free,
From Death's embrace, she longed not to see.

Her spirit bold, a flame that fiercely burned,
In quest of life's elixir, she discerned.
Through ancient texts and potions of old,
She sought the secret, a story yet untold.

But time, relentless, could not be denied,
And Death, relentless, stood by her side.
For all must succumb to the great unknown,
A truth she faced, though her spirit had grown.

Yet in her quest, she left a legacy behind,
A testament to dreams, to a seeking mind.
Her name engraved upon the sands of time,
A symbol of resilience, a soul sublime.

Here lies a woman who defied Death's cold grip,
In search of immortality, her journey's ship.
Though she may not have found what she pursued,
Her spirit lingers on, forever renewed.

In memory's embrace, her essence remains,
A beacon of hope, where immortality sustains.
Her epitaph, a reminder of dreams untold,
In her pursuit of life,
she found a story to behold.

WE SHALL ENDURE

Shadows cast by sorrow's endless reign,
I mourn the loss of friends and love's cruel sting.
Their absence haunts my soul with somber strain,
As darkness veils the melodies they sing.

In whispered echoes of their laughter's grace,
Their vibrant spirits linger in my mind.
But now, within this desolate embrace,
Their absence leaves an emptiness unkind.

Oh, bitter fate, that snatched them from my sight,
Leaving me yearning for their warm embrace.
Their memories, like ghosts, pierce through the night,
Leaving behind a void I cannot erase.

Yet, in this darkness, I shall strive to find
A glimmer of solace, a fragment of light,
To heal the wounds that dwell within my mind,
And cherish the love that once burned so bright.

Though sorrows weigh upon my weary heart,
I shall remember them, their spirits near,
For in their absence, they remain a part
Of who I am, forever held so dear.

And as I navigate this morbid gloom,
Their memory shall guide me through the night,
Each loss a reminder to seize life's bloom,
And treasure love, for it is our true light.

So, let this sonnet be a solemn ode,
To friends and love, departed from this earth.
May their essence linger, a timeless code,
Reminding us of the beauty of our birth.

Though darkness falls and sorrows may descend,
We shall endure, for love shall never end.

A Siders Alure

In shadows draped, a black widow weaves her web,
A femme fatale, with poison in her veins,
A deadly allure, her eyes a wicked ebb,
Beware the siren's call that veils her stains.

Her lover, entranced, falls into her snare,
Unaware of the venom lurking deep,
He surrenders, ignorant of her affair,
For in her touch, his soul begins to seep.

With delicate grace, she wraps him in silk,
A macabre dance of seduction and death,
Her crimson kiss, a fate of darkness ilk,
He draws his final breath, his final breath.

In mournful silence, she feasts on his remains,
A black widow's heart, where darkness forever reigns

Forevermore

From depths unknown, he rises to the night,
A figure pale, with eyes that burn like fire.
His heart now cold, devoid of mortal plight,
He seeks his love, consumed by dark desire.

Once mortal, bound by love's enduring thread,
Their passion, vibrant as a summer's bloom.
But fate unkind, it left him cold and dead,
And now he walks, a creature of the tomb.

Through moonlit streets, he wanders in despair,
In search of her, his one eternal mate.
To grant her life unending, he would dare,
To share with her the curse of his cruel fate.

Oh, bittersweet reunion in the gloom,
As he bestows on her the vampire's kiss,
Their love, immortal now, forever groomed,
In shadows deep, they find their eternal bliss.

No more shall mortal worries cloud their way,
Bound in darkness, where their desires soar.
As creatures of the night, they'll ever stay,
A love immortal, forevermore.

My Cruel Fate

In my chamber of despair, where darkness weaves,
Lies a tale of murder, hauntingly conceived.
I, once sane, now teeters on the edge,
Driven to madness by the spirits of the dead.

In the stillness of the night, they whisper my name,
Their haunting cries echo, fueling my flame.
Tormented by remorse, their eyes pierce my soul,
I seeks a twisted solace, a demonic control.

Summoning the shadows, I call forth the abyss,
Beckoning demons to rid me of this nemesis.
Their vile forms emerge, from the depths they arise,
To aid me in my quest, as darkness fills the skies.

But the spirits, relentless, refuse to be silenced,
Their cries grow louder, their presence undiminished.
They torment my thoughts, my dreams filled with dread,
For I am bound to the remorse of the dead.

In chambers cloaked in shadows, I makes my stand,
Confronting the ghosts, the blood on my hands.
But the demons, deceitful, reveal their true intent,
To claim my soul, my sanity rent.

A battle ensues, a clash of dark and light,
As I fight against the spectral might.
The demons, relentless, tear at my mind,
While the spirits, undying, seek retribution in kind.

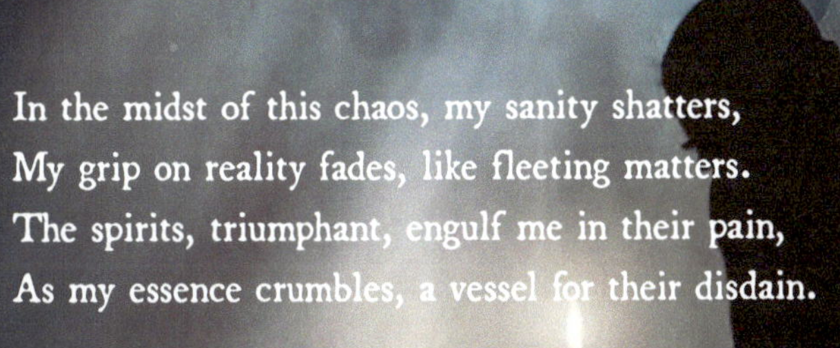

In the midst of this chaos, my sanity shatters,
My grip on reality fades, like fleeting matters.
The spirits, triumphant, engulf me in their pain,
As my essence crumbles, a vessel for their disdain.

I a once sane man, now lost to the abyss,
A victim of my deeds, the specters' endless hiss.
No demons or incantations can break my fall,
For the haunting echoes of the dead conquer all.

And so the tale concludes, in madness and despair,
A murderer consumed by the spirits' relentless glare.
In the chamber of despair, I meets my cruel fate,
A puppet of darkness, lost in eternal debate.

DUALITY OF A CAT

In a moonlight haze, where worlds entwine,
An ethereal being, both yours and mine,
A cat of wonder, a mystical grace,
Existing between two realms' embrace.

One moment, a friend, gentle and kind,
A furry companion, soul intertwined,
Meowing melodies, a comforting purr,
A presence of solace, soft sweet allure.

But then, a shift in the midnight air,
Eyes gleaming, glowing, a spectral stare,
From this mortal realm, it fades away,
A spirit of the night, swift and fey.

With sharp claws and fangs, it takes its flight,
Silent and swift, through the veil of night,
A hunter, relentless, it seeks its prey,
In the shadowed realms where darkness holds sway.

Between worlds it slips, a phantom unseen,
Navigating realms where mysteries convene,
Its sleek form dances, elusive and rare,
Leaving no trace, but a whisper of air.

A paradox unveiled, both real and ethereal,
A creature existing in the mystical surreal,
Within its essence, realms interlace,
A beautiful friend, a spirit of grace.

Oh, mystic cat, you hold the key,
To secrets of realms beyond what we see,
In your eyes, the wisdom of the ages unfurls,
As you navigate between both worlds.

So, cherish the moments when it draws near,
For its presence brings joy, banishes fear,
Embrace the duality, the enigmatic blend,
Of a cat, a spirit, a forever-fleeting friend.

IN SEARCH OF BRAINS

In a world bereft of life's vibrant gleam,

A zombie roams, consumed by endless thirst.

Its hunger rages like a twisted dream,

Yet, finds no solace in this realm accursed.

Its vacant eyes, devoid of human spark,

Seek brains to feast upon, a gruesome plight.

But in this modern age, a world so stark,

Thoughts and intellect vanish from its sight.

Where once were minds with knowledge to explore,

Now dwells a shallow void, an empty well.

The zombie's desperate quest forevermore,

To sate its appetite, a fruitless spell.

A tragic figure trapped in limbo's snare,

In search of brains, it finds a world laid bare.

WHERE DREAMS COLLID

In ages past, a tale I weave,

Of love and loss, and hearts that grieve.

Where towering castle stood so grand,

A tragic fate, I now command.

'Twas in the days of yore, you see,

When love was mine, and joy ran free.

My love, fair and full of grace,

Her radiant smile lit up the space.

We wandered hand in hand, so bright,

Through halls of stone, kissed by moonlight.

In every corner, love did dwell,

Within the castle's ancient spell.

But fate, unkind, upon us frowned,

And tragedy soon swept around.

Upon the wall, so high and steep,

Where dreams collided, love would weep.

One fateful day, my love so dear,

Slipped from the top, a soul to sear.

She tumbled down, her life to end,

My heart shattered, no solace to lend.

Years passed me by, with sorrow's weight,

Until I dared to challenge fate.

Returning to that castle's keep,

In search of answers, and souls to meet.

The sun sank low, the day grew dim,

I reached the wall where life was grim.

And there, as twilight's hues unfurled,

My love's ghost, my heart unfurled.

She stood upon that very ledge,

Her ethereal form upon the edge.

Her spectral eyes, a mournful gaze,

A wistful echo of bygone days.

With trembling steps, I drew her near,
To seek the truth, to calm my fear.
But as I delved into the air,
A raven perched, its eerie stare.

Its onyx eyes pierced through my soul,
As if it knew, the tale untold.
Then, with a flap, it took to flight,
Guiding me toward the fading light.

With hesitant resolve, I peered below,
And felt a touch, a spectral blow.
Hands upon my trembling back,
They pushed me forth, no turning back.

I plunged into the abyss of air,
The castle walls, a last despair.
But as I fell, no fear did bloom,
For in death's embrace, I found my tomb.

Now reunited, souls entwined,
With my love, forever I'll find.
In death's realm, where shadows meet,
Our love shall eternally repeat.

No more to feel sorrow's sting,
No more to hear the raven sing.
In the castle's depths, our spirits soar,
A tragic tale forevermore.

WHERE DREAMS COLLID

From Shallow Graves

On the edge of twilight's embrace, the girl awaits,
Her heart aflutter, her soul aflame with hope,
As shadows dance upon the lonely gate,
She longs for friends, but finds no kindly trope.

With every passing moment, time drags on,
Each tick a pang of sorrow in her chest,
Her laughter fades, like whispers in the dawn,
Alas, her birthday joy remains unblessed.

No footsteps echo down the empty street,
No voices sing, no mirthful greetings sound,
Her heartache grows, her disappointment deep,
In solitude, her spirit feels unbound.

But in her desperation's icy clutch,
She turns to darkness, seeks a morbid touch.

With desperate hands, she ventures through the gloom,
Into the graveyard, where the dead abide,
Where tombstones loom and silence finds its bloom,
She seeks companions, cold and deathly tied.

Beneath the silver moon's soft, mournful glow,
She digs with frenzied fervor in the earth,
Her fingers graced with the cemetery's woe,
As soil and secrets mingle in rebirth.

From shallow graves, she reaps her birthday guests,
Their pallid forms, no longer bound by death,
Their hollow eyes, like somber lanterns, rest,
To celebrate, with bated, spectral breath.

She places crowns of wilted blooms on heads,
Their tattered garments kissed by autumn's sighs,
They stand as shadows, mingling with the dead,
Their presence bringing her a macabre prize.

As moonlight dances on their lifeless frames,
They twirl and spin, in waltzing elegance,
Their bony fingers grasp, eternal games,
Their eerie chorus sings, a haunting resonance.

The midnight hour, a reminder of their fate,
Draws near, as fleeting as a ghostly breath,
And with a heavy heart, she contemplates,
To bid farewell to her spectral guests of death.

Alone once more, her steps grow faint,
With whispered gratitude, a ghostly saint,
She walks away, her heart alight,
Having found solace in the dead of night.

For in the graveyard's desolate embrace,
She found a birthday celebration, full of grace,
Where the departed souls, with her, did play,
A macabre tribute to her special day.

In Moonlights Gleam

Upon the ancient woods, in moonlight's gleam,

I tread with caution, whispers on the air,

Where shadows dance, and secrets softly stream.

A wolf's lament breaks silence with a scream,

A haunting call, a warning to beware,

Upon the ancient woods, in moonlight's gleam.

Through silent groves, where ancient spirits dream,

A river's mirror reflects the lunar glare,

Where shadows dance, and secrets softly stream.

Behold! A fair woman, grace supreme,

In a crimson gown, a vision beyond compare,

Upon the ancient woods, in moonlight's gleam.

Beside her, a horned man, a curious team,

In revelry, they laugh and drink their share,

Where shadows dance, and secrets softly stream.

But swift as thought, the horned man's departure seemed,

Leaving behind but memories to share,

Upon the ancient woods, in moonlight's gleam.

A pact forged with the devil, it would seem,
A dance of darkness, forbidden and rare,
Where shadows dance, and secrets softly stream.

Forever etched in mind, a vivid theme,
That night I saw the devil and the maiden fair,
Upon the ancient woods, in moonlight's gleam,
Where shadows dance, and secrets softly stream.

A Desolate Creature

Liquid shadows' dance by moonlit streams,
A haunting presence, lurking, it seems.
Outside my window, by the river's embrace,
There dwells a creature, yearning for a trace.

I lay in bed, consumed by dread,
A prisoner of fear, eyes tightly shut, I tread.
Its mournful moans, a chilling refrain,
Echos of anguish, a tormenting strain.

What dwells beyond, in the watery abyss,
A visage unseen, shrouded in mist?
Is it a specter, with ghostly breath,
Or a forgotten soul, sentenced to death?

The river whispers tales untold,
Of secrets kept within its fold.
Beneath the surface, darkness thrives,
A desolate creature, no longer alive.

Each night it moans, a mournful plea,
Beckoning me closer, tempting me to see.
But I remain hidden, my gaze averted,
For what awaits, my soul is alerted.

Its cries grow louder, like a funeral dirge,
A haunting melody, my fears do surge.
The weight of its presence, heavy in the air,
A specter of despair, tormenting and unfair.

In dreams, it visits, a malevolent guise,
A formless specter with hollow eyes.
It whispers of sorrow, of anguish and pain,
As I lie defenseless, in its relentless domain.

Oh, wretched creature, cursed and forlorn,
What twisted fate has left you torn?
A prisoner of the river's cold embrace,
Condemned to wander, with no solace or grace.

Yet, I remain in bed, forever concealed,
Refusing to witness the truth unrevealed.
For ignorance, though unsettling, brings respite,
And the horrors outside shall not invade my night.

So I close my ears to its haunting cries,
And veil my eyes from its ghostly guise.
A prisoner in my own fortress of fear,
Trapped in the presence that lingers so near.

And as the river flows, forever it moans,
Its mournful lament, an eternal drone.
But locked away in my sheltered bed,
I choose ignorance, instead of facing dread

a Mysterious girl

As I ponder the shadows, where sorrows reside,

I sought solace in darkness, where pain could subside.

To my local dance club, I made my way,

A sanctuary of melancholy, where hearts would sway.

Amidst the dimly lit hall, where souls were lost,

I drowned my woes in a chalice, bitterness embossed.

And there, in the midst of the somber dance,

A vision emerged, captivating my glance.

A Gothic maiden, dressed in ebony attire,

Moved with elegance, consumed by the fire.

To the haunting melodies of The Cure's embrace,

She danced in solace, transcending time and space.

Our eyes entwined, in a moment's connection,

A smile she bestowed, igniting affection.

My heart leaped within, an ember ablaze,

Hope and intrigue mingled in an enigmatic haze

Approaching with trepidation, I ventured near,

In her presence, a mystique that fueled my fear.

Through conversations profound, the night slipped away,

Unraveling mysteries and secrets, as shadows held sway.

Hand in hand, we emerged from the club's embrace,
Under moonlit skies, we traversed, in tranquil grace.
Yet, as moonbeams danced upon her ethereal frame,
Her form grew translucent, fading, as if just a wisp, a name.

Bewildered, I questioned, "Where are you bound?"
Her lips moved in response, but silence was found.
In an ephemeral instant, she vanished from my sight,
Leaving me alone, lost in the desolate night.

Returning to the club, my heart filled with despair,
Searching in vain, amidst the gloom and empty air.
But the mystirous girl, a phantom of the night,
Never graced the dance floor with her ethereal light.

In the depths of my longing, I'm left to ponder,
Was she a figment of my melancholic wander?
A fleeting dream, a specter, conjured by intoxicated whims,
A haunting illusion, stitched from moonlight's hymns.

Thus, I tread the cobblestone path of despair,
Haunted by the memory of a love so rare.
Forever wondering, in the realm of the surreal,
If she, my mystirous girl, was ever truly real.

The Final Gasp

Beneath a sky of ashen gray,
A symphony of chaos starts to play.
Whispers echo through the air,
Foretelling doom, the end so near.

The oceans rise, their fury unleashed,
As tidal waves crash, shores are breached.
Mountains crumble, quaking in despair,
The Earth's foundation stripped and bare.

The winds howl with a mournful cry,
Tearing through cities, bidding goodbye.
The structures we built, once so grand,
Reduced to rubble, dust in the sand.

Flames devour the once vibrant land,
Consuming all with an eager hand.
Forests ablaze, their emerald hues,
Now charred remnants, lost and bruised.

The cries of creatures fill the void,
Their homes destroyed, their spirits toyed.
From soaring birds to humble bee,
All life surrenders to destiny.

Yet in this chaos, a silence looms,
A glimpse of beauty amidst the tombs.
Hand in hand, souls find solace there,
Love's final stand, a bond to bear.

As darkness falls, the stars align,
A cosmic dance, a final sign.
The universe weeps, its final tear,
A requiem for a world held dear.

The end is nigh, the tale is told,
The tapestry of life begins to fold.
Yet in the ashes, a spark remains,
A flicker of hope, free from the chains.

For from destruction, new seeds are sown,
A chance for a world yet unknown.
So let us dream of a brighter day,
As the old world gracefully fades away.

Ode To The Moon

Oh haunting orb, mistress of the night,
In your enigmatic glow, darkness takes flight,
A specter in the sky, your presence forebodes,
A tale of eerie secrets and forbidding roads.

In the shadows, you cast a ghostly gleam,
An accomplice to nightmares, a harbinger of dream,
You illuminate the realm where horrors reside,
Unveiling the secrets that humanity hides.

Beneath your gaze, the world turns ashen,
As spirits awaken and specters fasten,
Upon the hearts of the lost and forlorn,
A wretched dance of despair, a haunting morn.

Oh Moon, you bear witness to the macabre,
The restless souls and the cursed, so sombre,
In your pallid light, their stories unfold,
Dark deeds and tragedies, untold and cold.

You summon the creatures that lurk in the night,
Those born of shadows, hidden from sight,
The werewolves howl and vampires arise,
As the moon's curse takes hold, darkness mesmerize.

In the graveyard's embrace, your light cascades,
Revealing tombstones, where death's legacy pervades,
Ghosts whisper their tales, lost in time,
Their mournful laments, a melancholic rhyme.

Oh Moon, your aura taints the celestial sphere,
With an ethereal chill that awakens fear,
Your enigmatic face, a mask so serene,
Hiding the horrors that lie in-between.

In this nocturnal realm, where nightmares breed,
You reign supreme, the queen of the seed,
A mesmerizing mistress of the macabre,
Your haunting glow, a sinister saboteur.

So here's my ode to you, Moon of dread,
As you cast your spell upon the undead,
May your eerie light forever dance,
In the dark recesses of our chilling trance.

Dedicated to Lyria. . .

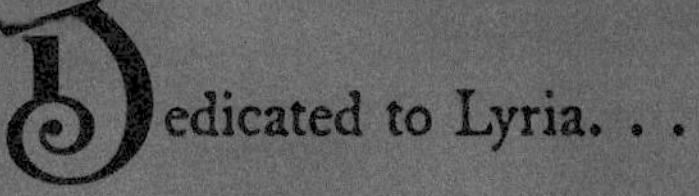